# Good Friends Make Life Bearable

Paintings by *Susan Rios*

HARVEST HOUSE™ PUBLISHERS
EUGENE, OREGON

# Good Friends Make Life Bearable

Copyright © 2003 by Harvest House Publishers
Eugene, Oregon 97402

ISBN 0-7369-1102-2

Original artwork © Susan Rios. Licensed by Art Impressions, Canoga Park, CA. For more information regarding artwork featured in this book, please contact:

Art Impressions
9035-A Eton Avenue
Canoga Park, CA 91304-1616
(818) 700-8541

Design and production by Garborg Design Works, Minneapolis, Minnesota

**Printed in Hong Kong**

03 04 05 06 07 08 09 10 11 / NG / 10 9 8 7 6 5 4 3 2 1

## To My Dear Friend

_____

### Love,

_____

$Love$ bears all things, believes all things,
hopes all things, endures all things.
Love never fails.

THE BOOK OF 1 CORINTHIANS

$\mathcal{A}$ge simply doesn't enter into it! The older the friend, the more he is valued, particularly when he shows so visibly the characteristics that we all look for in friends. You have only to look at a genuine teddy's face to see at once the loyalty, common sense, and above all, dependability behind it.

PETER BULL

What one loves in childhood stays in the heart forever.

MARY JO PUTNEY

Friendship...is both genuine and spontaneous.

MARCUS CICERO

*I am beginning to
learn that it is the
sweet, simple things of
life which are the real
ones after all.*

LAURA INGALLS WILDER

My teddy was there when I had no friends to play with, no one to talk to, no one to share my little woes or my big joys. He looked constant and was constant. He never aged, no matter how tattered he became. His smell was the smell of my years as a boy, and he alone knew everything. Now, when I see him on the shelf, he is like my flesh and my soul—older, worn, but still full of happiness.

ROBERT KUNCIOV

Even though there is a rip in your

teddy bear, his love will not fall out.

EVE FRANCES GIGLIOTTI

Our sweetest

experiences of

affection are

meant to point us

to that realm

which is the real

and endless home

of the heart.

HENRY WARD BEECHER

A cheerful heart is good medicine.

THE BOOK OF PROVERBS

There is a treasure chest inside of me filled
with thoughts of you. In my quiet moments I
open it and cherish again the friendship we share.

Teddy bears are
wonderful reminders
for us to have soft
edges, be full of
love and trust,
and always be ready
for a hug.

Friendships are what our dreams are made of.

We hold onto each other with its binding love.

We stand close to each other, hand in hand,

Showing each other we understand.

Some friends may come and go,

But you are the truest friend I know.

ELSA MAXWELL

A bear teaches us that if the heart is true,

it doesn't matter much if an ear drops off.

HELEN EXLEY

The best kind of friend is the kind you can
then walk away feeling like it was the best

When a child loves you for a long, long time, not just to play with, but *really* loves you, then you become real. Generally, by the time you are real, most of your hair has been loved off, and you get loose in the joints and very shabby. But these things don't matter at all, because once you are real, you can't be ugly—except to people who don't understand.

MARGERY WILLIAMS
*Velveteen Rabbit*

sit on a porch swing with, never say a word, conversation that you ever had.

ANONYMOUS

# In my friend, I find a second self.

ISABEL NORTON

*The growth of
friendship might
be a lifelong affair.*

SARAH ORNE JEWETT

Teddy bears, with their plush, huggable bodies and amiable expressions, seem to possess an endearing quality of listening without judging. They bring out the best in us by fostering feelings of comfort, trust and love. Teddies, with their soothing faces, help the young and the old—and those somewhere in between—get through difficult times of sickness and need.

BO NILES
*Country Bears*

$\mathcal{I}$ cannot even imagine where I
would be today were it not for that
handful of friends who have given
me a heart full of joy. Let's face it,
friends make life a lot more fun.

CHARLES R. SWINDOLL

Never forget me, because if $\mathcal{I}$
thought you would, $\mathcal{I}$'d never leave.

A.A. MILNE

SusanRios

*The person who tries to live alone will not succeed as a human being. His heart withers if it does not answer another heart. His mind shrinks away if he hears only the echoes of his own thoughts and finds no other inspiration.*

PEARL S. BUCK

*A man who has friends must himself be friendly, But there is a friend who sticks closer than a brother.*

THE BOOK OF PROVERBS

What is it about this inanimate object of fur and stuffing that makes it so hard to part with? As children, we were acutely aware of just how much our bears loved us, and we filled their ears with our daily doings and deepest confidences. How could one grow up and not take along this dearest of companions?

SARAH McCLENNAN

So wherever I am, there's always Pooh,

There's always Pooh and Me.

"What would I do?" I said to Pooh,

"If it wasn't for you," and Pooh said: "True,

It isn't much fun for One, but Two

Can stick together," says Pooh, says he.

"That's how it is," says Pooh.

A.A. MILNE

*You do not know how much they mean to me, my friends, and how,*

*how rare and strange it is, to find in a life composed so much of odds*

*and ends…to find a friend who has these qualities, who has, and gives*

*those qualities upon which friendship lives. How much it means that*

*I say this to you—without these friendships—life, what a nightmare!*

T.S. ELIOT

Ah, how good it feels! The hand of an old friend.

HENRY WADSWORTH LONGFELLOW

Friendship is a chain of gold

Shaped in God's all perfect mold,

Each link a smile, a laugh, a tear,

A grip of the hand, a word of cheer.

As steadfast as the ages roll

Binding closer soul to soul;

No matter how far, or heavy the load—

Sweet is the journey on friendship's road.

J.B. DOWNE

I awoke this morning with devout thanksgiving
for my friends, the old and the new.

RALPH WALDO EMERSON

*H*ere is Edward Bear, coming downstairs now, bump, bump, on the back of his head, behind Christopher Robin. It is, as far as he knows, the only way of coming downstairs, but sometimes he feels that there really is another way, if only he could stop bumping a moment and think of it. And then, he feels that perhaps there isn't. Anyhow, here he is at the bottom, and ready to be introduced to you. Winnie-the-Pooh.

A.A. MILNE

*Be completely humble and gentle; be patient, bearing with one another in love.*

THE BOOK OF EPHESIANS

## Friendship is love refined.

SUSANNAH CENTLIVRE

My old friend

Makes my hopes of clearer light,

And my faith of surer sight,

And my soul a purer white,

My old friend.

JAMES WHITCOMB RILEY

## Everyone smiles in the same language.

OLD PROVERB

*There is nothing on this earth more to be prized than true friendship.*

ST. THOMAS AQUINAS

*In a world where everyone seems to be larger and louder than yourself, it is very comforting to have a small, quiet companion.*

PETER GRAY

*Friends are the sunshine of life.*

JOHN HAY

# There's no friend like someone who has known you since you were five.

ANNE STEVENSON

If you could look into my heart

And see your image there;

You'd like the sunny loveliness

Your goodness makes it wear.

MARY ELIZABETH NEWELL

An encouraging friend is a lifeline to steady a floundering
heart, to bring sunshine to a cloudy day,
and to deliver a blessing just looking for a place to land.

SUSAN DUKE

An experienced teddy bear brings with him a lifetime of knowledge and experience; the wisdom of silence and the stillness in moments of great turmoil. The long-suffering patience that is learned when belonging to a child who is coming of age, and coping with the bewilderment that this period of time can bring, is what he does best. The experienced bear has seen life through the heart and eyes of a child grown to adulthood and perhaps even accompanied that adult all the way to the end of the road.

TED MENTON

SusanRios

It must be eleven years now since Kathy went for a walk with the cleaning lady and came home with a teddy bear she'd won in a raffle they'd passed.

He's still going strong. He's no longer pink fuzz (or was he blue when he was new?) but grey homespun, and his left arm has a red patch and his glass eyes have long since been swallowed by the current dog. He's a heartbreaking sight. But he's a great traveler, Teddy.

He's been to California, Cape Canaveral and Key West; to Colombia, Cuba and Jamaica; to Connecticut, Cape Cod and Killooeet Camp. He's a regular Columbus. He's traveled more in his eleven years than I have in 39. I've never traveled parcel post; Teddy has, in a box with a hole punched on the bottom so he could breathe.

Teddy was not only a good companion and perfect bed-mate; he was the quickest way to a chambermaid's heart. The sternest of them would push her way into the girls' room, stiffen at the laundry and mutter "Slobs" in Schweitzerdeutsch, only to melt into fondue at the sight of Teddy snuggled among the rumpled sheets. He turned bed-making into a privilege. He got a ribbon on his neck in Paris, two pillows in Athens and a nightgown made out of a hand towel in Rome.

VIOLET WEINGARTEN
*You Can Take Them with You*

$\mathcal{A}$nd great and numerous as are the blessings of friendship, this certainly is the sovereign one, that it gives us bright hopes for the future and forbids weakness and despair. In the face of a true friend a man sees as it were a second self. So that where his friend is he is; if his friend be rich, he is not poor; though he be weak, his friend's strength is his; and in his friend's life he enjoys a second life after his own is finished.

MARCUS CICERO

*A friend should bear his friend's infirmities.*

WILLIAM SHAKESPEARE

Long before I grew up, my teddy bear taught me what love really meant—being there when you're needed.

JIM NELSON

'Tis the privilege of friendship to talk nonsense, and have her nonsense respected.

CHARLES LAMB

All love that has not friendship for its base,

Is like a mansion built upon the sand.

ELLA WHEELER WILCOX

SusanRios

*B*e courteous to all, but
intimate with few, and let
those few be well tried
before you give them your
confidence. True friendship
is a plant of slow growth,
and must undergo and
withstand the shocks of
adversity before it is
entitled to the appellation.

GEORGE WASHINGTON

*Seeds of kindness, goodwill, and human understanding, planted
in fertile soil, spring up into deathless friendships, big deeds of
worth, and a memory that will not soon fade...*

GEORGE MATTHEW ADAMS

# Bear with each other and forgive. . . .one another.

THE BOOK OF COLOSSIANS

A teddy bear is a faithful friend

You can pick him up at either end.

His fur is the color of breakfast toast,

And he's always there when you need him most.

AUTHOR UNKNOWN

*The purpose of friendship is to have one dearer to me than myself,*

*and for the saving of whose life I would gladly lay down my own.*

SENECA

W hat can be more delightful than to have someone to whom you can say everything with the same absolute confidence as to yourself?

MARCUS CICERO

*Every friend is like a flower*
*in life that is admired*
*for its exquisite beauty and*
*God-given design.*

GINNY HOBSON

Teddy bear hugs are like chocolate:

You can never get enough.

AUTHOR UNKNOWN

SusanRios

47

Many a heart learns to love
from its first teddy bear.